Essay On Gothic Architecture: With Various Plans And Drawings For Churches

John Henry Hopkins

Nabu Public Domain Reprints:

You are holding a reproduction of an original work published before 1923 that is in the public domain in the United States of America, and possibly other countries. You may freely copy and distribute this work as no entity (individual or corporate) has a copyright on the body of the work. This book may contain prior copyright references, and library stamps (as most of these works were scanned from library copies). These have been scanned and retained as part of the historical artifact.

This book may have occasional imperfections such as missing or blurred pages, poor pictures, errant marks, etc. that were either part of the original artifact, or were introduced by the scanning process. We believe this work is culturally important, and despite the imperfections, have elected to bring it back into print as part of our continuing commitment to the preservation of printed works worldwide. We appreciate your understanding of the imperfections in the preservation process, and hope you enjoy this valuable book.

ESSAY ON Gothic Architecture,
WITH VARIOUS PLANS AND DRAWINGS For Churches,

Designed chiefly for the use of

THE CLERGY.

THE NEW YORK
PUBLIC LIBRARY
399223A
ASTOR, LENOX AND
TILDEN FOUNDATIONS
R 1928 L

ESSAY

ON

GOTHIC ARCHITECTURE,

WITH VARIOUS PLANS AND DRAWINGS

FOR CHURCHES:

DESIGNED CHIEFLY FOR THE USE OF

THE CLERGY.

BY JOHN HENRY HOPKINS, D. D.
Bishop of the Protestant Episcopal Church in the Diocese of Vermont.

BURLINGTON:
PRINTED BY SMITH & HARRINGTON.
1836.

Entered according to act of Congress, in the year 1836,
by SMITH & HARRINGTON,
in the Clerk's office of the District Court, for the District of Vermont.

PREFACE.

In presenting the following work to those who are interested in Church Architecture, the author is sensible that he is liable, amongst professional architects especially, to the charge of presumption, for meddling with a science which he cannot be supposed to understand. Perhaps the best mode of defending himself against this accusation, and of making a true apology for the book itself, will be to state the simple facts which gave rise to the undertaking.

About the latter part of the year 1823, the author entered upon his first ministerial charge, in the city of Pittsburgh, Pennsylvania; and the blessing granted to his humble labors soon excited his congregation to attempt the erection of a new church, which was designed to be in every respect superior to the building then occupied as their house of worship. The first point which presented itself, was, of course, the adoption of a plan; and amongst a variety of drawings produced for the occasion, the author saw none which satisfied him. His early youth had been passed in more than ordinary familiarity with the Fine Arts, but, except as a topic of taste and general science, he had no knowledge of Architecture. Admiring, however, the Gothic style above all others, and seeing nothing in the drawings presented which accorded with it, he took up the pencil himself, and tried to embody his own vague conceptions in a regular form.

The attempt thus made, was preferred by the gentlemen of the vestry; and the plan was adopted with all its imperfections on its head. But the author was conscious of his deficiencies in this new department; and felt himself bound, as far as possible, to supply them. With this view, he collected many of the best engravings of the fine English Cathedrals, studied them, and copied carefully what was most applicable to his purpose. And in this stage of his labors he was aided beyond his hopes by the acquaintance of a European architect* who just then settled in his neighborhood, and kindly loaned to him the valuable works of Britton, in which he found a real treasury of taste and information. The result was the completion of Trinity Church, Pittsburgh, in a manner which at least exceeded the expectations of all concerned; and drew upon the author, from that time forward, more applications for church plans, than he found it either convenient or practicable to furnish.

In the progress of his subsequent observation, he discovered that even several of our large cities were chiefly indebted to the voluntary labours of amateurs for their Gothic architecture; that with some rare exceptions, professional architects had paid but little attention to the Gothic style, or to the peculiar structure of churches; and that the works most easy of access on architecture in general, gave few if any instructions on the subject. While, throughout the country at large, he saw every where the most uncouth combinations of the Gothic arch and battlement, with columns, entablatures, and pediments, of the Grecian order; clearly proving the general deficiency in this department of ecclesiastical taste, and calling for some attempt, however humble, to establish a better standard.

Under these circumstances, and stimulated by the repeated calls made upon him for plans of churches by his clerical brethren, the author commenced the following essay several years ago; and committed the greater part of the drawings to the lithographic press, during his residence near Boston. Availing himself of the excellent aids which he found in the Athenæum of that city, and devoting to the work the chief portion of his leisure hours, he found it grow almost insensibly upon his hands, to a size which seemed, at length, to warrant publication. He puts it forth, however, not presuming that it can teach the professional architect, nor claiming for it the rank of a regular and systematic treatise; but as the essay of a mere amateur, only intended to be of service, where better guides are not at hand. And above all, his desire and hope, are that it may induce our rising

---

* John Behan, Esq. a gentleman of great skill in his profession, of whose services the author would gladly have availed himself, if the funds of the church had justified him.

clergy to give attention to a subject which peculiarly concerns themselves; and which must, in the nature of things, be principally committed to their management in a country like ours; where the assistance of professional architects cannot often be obtained, and where, in a majority of cases, the funds provided for the building of our churches so seldom warrant the employing them.

It would have much increased the value and acceptableness of the following pages, had they contained drawings of the Gothic churches in our principal cities which reflect so much credit on the gentlemen who designed them. But the author omitted them on purpose, for two reasons: first, because he considers the plans of these edifices as being the property of others; and secondly, because one of the benefits which he should rejoice to derive from the publication of the present work, is the provoking some of his qualified brethren to put forth a better one.

The author cannot dismiss these prefatory remarks without adverting to the possibility, that some of his Christian brethren may regret the appearance of his book on another ground; as thinking that his whole time is little enough for the due performance of the higher and more strictly spiritual duties of his responsible office, and that the care of the outward edifice might be better left to other hands.

To this he will only say, that every thing connected with the service of the Most High, is worthy the attention of his ministry, and indeed, devolves upon them, as forming a part of their peculiar office, which, if they will not take pains to understand, they cannot expect that other men will. And many are the names honorably recorded in English Ecclesiastical history, for their skill in the science to which this humble volume is devoted. The famous William of Wykeham, bishop of Winchester, in the reign of Edward III, Archbishop Chichelé, Alcock, bishop of Ely, Richard Beauchamp, bishop of Salisbury, who was appointed Master and Surveyor of the works, by Edward IV, in the rebuilding St. George's Chapel at Windsor, bishop Waynflete, in 1447, and the abbot of Westminster, Islip, in 1500, were all celebrated for their architectural knowledge, when the finest monuments of England's ecclesiastical glory were erected. But far beyond these—Moses, the leader of Israel, took charge of all the details of the earthly sanctuary—Bezaleel the son of Uri, was called specially and filled with the Spirit of God (Exod. xxxi. 1,

2,) to make the work belonging to the tabernacle. Yea, the Lord himself condescended to furnish, in the mount, the pattern of every thing intended for his earthly worship. On a similar principle, David and Solomon, the most distinguished kings of Israel, employed themselves, the one in preparing for, and the other in erecting, the Temple at Jerusalem: and the volume of heavenly wisdom—the blessed word of God—is occupied to a considerable extent, in the description of each minute appendage of his sanctuary. Most unscriptural, therefore, would be the censure—most misplaced the affectation of regret, which should seek to dissuade the clergy from applying themselves to the art of erecting the earthly houses of God in a fitting and appropriate manner. The author would be among the first to maintain the superior claims of instruction, and devotion, and pastoral government, over every other branch of ministerial accomplishment. But he is fully persuaded, that a moderate degree of industry and application will find time for them all. He cannot understand, why the clergy should not possess a competent familiarity with the whole range of subjects connected with their sacred calling; nor has he ever been able to see how a reasonable knowledge and zeal in the construction of the outward tabernacle, should lessen their energy and success in the preaching of the Gospel.

BURLINGTON, VT. MARCH, 1836.

CHAPTER I.

ON THE ORIGIN OF THE GOTHIC STYLE OF ARCHITECTURE.

The Gothic style of architecture has long possessed a high rank in the estimate of ecclesiastical taste, and has drawn forth no small share of erudition in the various attempts made by European writers, to trace its derivation. Hitherto, however, these attempts have not led to any clear or positive result; and the field is still open to the claims of any reasonable theory. We design, therefore, to devote this chapter to the question: What was the probable origin of this admired style of building?

The distinguishing features of the Gothic style seem to consist in two particulars—the effect of the perpendicular line, and the terminating the various parts in a point. It must be understood, however, that we are not speaking of the Gothic style in its application to castles or colleges, where its true principles are obliged to give way to the superior claims of strength and convenience. Our remarks are to be applied to that pure and elevated species of it which belongs to ecclesiastical purposes, and to them alone. In this—when exhibited in its best specimens—we find that all the upper horizontal lines are broken into battlements, while the multiplied perpendicular lines of the buttresses, crowned with pinnacles diminishing to a point, the mullioned windows, and the slender clustered pillars, lead the eye of the beholder upwards; causing, by a kind of physical association, an impression of sublimity more exalted than any other sort of architecture can produce.

Now it is here that we find the superiority of the Gothic over the Grecian style, for ecclesiastical purposes. The Gothic, breaking the horizontal line, and leading the eye upwards till its pinnacles vanish in the sky, seems adapted, by an easy correspondence, to the offices of that blessed religion, which takes the heart from the contemplation of earth, and directs it to its heavenly inheritance. While the Grecian, with its lengthened colonnades and its horizontal extension, running in lines parallel with the ground, seems suited, by its characteristic expression, to secular objects and pursuits. Hence we should recommend the Grecian and Roman architecture for all buildings designed for legislative, judicial, commercial, civic, or merely scientific purposes; but wherever the spiritual interests of our race are to be the primary concern, the elevated solemnity of the Gothic style is far more appropriate.

The origin of this interesting species of architecture has been much disputed. Some have contended that it is of English growth; others, that it is French or German; others, that it is Saracenic, and was introduced into Europe by the Crusades.* Of these opinions the latter has by far the greatest plausibility: as may

---

* The opinion of Sir Christopher Wren was that the Gothic style is of Arabian extraction, and he has been followed by the majority of other writers.

Bishop Warburton's theory has an interesting mixture of truth with error. 'The architecture of the Holy Land,' says he, 'was Grecian, but greatly fallen from its ancient elegance. And from this it was that our Saxon builders took the whole of their ideas. But when the Goths conquered Spain, through emulation of the Saracens, they struck out a new species of architecture upon original principles, and ideas much nobler than what had given birth even to classic magnificence. For this northern people having been accustomed to worship the Deity in groves, when their new religion required covered edifices, they ingeniously projected to make them resemble groves,'——' and with what skill and success they executed the project by the assistance of Saracen architects, whose exotic style of building very luckily suited their purpose, appears from hence, that no attentive observer ever viewed a regular avenue of well grown trees intermingling their branches overhead, but it presently put him in mind of the long vista through the Gothic cathedral.' This notion of the learned Bishop, that a new style of building could thus arise in the 10th century, upon an original model, without any record of the design or the name of the designer, is certainly, to say the least, a violent presumption. But his idea of a grove is beautiful and just; only that instead of referring it, on a mere conjecture, to an ordinary grove, and to the middle ages for its origin, it seems much more reasonable to trace it to the palm trees, which we know were represented, within and without, in the celebrated

plainly appear from the following considerations. First, because it is acknowledged that no specimens of pure and tasteful design in Europe, can be traced farther back than the twelfth century, a little after the first crusade. Secondly, because there is abundant evidence to prove that the ecclesiastics were the architects, and often the very workmen, by whom those splendid edifices were erected, which are the admiration of the civilized world to this day. Thirdly, because the architecture of Palestine and of the East generally, displays all the distinguishing characteristics of the Gothic style—the pointed arch—the ogee—the pinnacle—the fretted tracery—the lofty minaret—the panel formed by segments of circles—the ornamental foliage: and fourthly, because multitudes of abbots, friars, priests, and monks, accompanied the armies of the cross to the very regions of this peculiar architecture. It is an obvious inference from these premises, that the clergy of that

---

temple of Solomon. Probably Bishop Warburton was influenced by the term *Gothic*, which is now generally conceded to be a nickname of reproach, instead of a note of history.

The notion of the poet Gray is strangely absurd, that the buildings of Turkey, Persia, and the East Indies, are plainly 'corruptions of the Greek architecture, broke into little parts indeed, and covered with small ornaments, but in taste very distinguishable from what we call Gothic.' And he asks 'Who ever saw a Gothic cupola? It is a thing plainly of Greek extraction.' Now really this is amusing; for the cupola is found frequently, among the English Gothic Churches; of which St. George's Chapel and King's College Chapel are familiar instances. Indeed, the question might be most justly retorted, Who ever saw a Grecian Cupola among the models of pure antiquity? The Cupola was added to the genuine Grecian style, by mixing it with ideas borrowed from the East.

A French writer in the 'Souvenirs du Musée des Monumens Français' so late as the year 1826, shews the doubtful state of this question very clearly by these questions; 'Le style' says he, 'qui, dans le onzieme siècle, fit oublier l'architecture Carlovingiaque, fut il creé par des artistes descendans des anciens *Goths*, et doit il, pour cette raison, être appellé *Gothique?* Dut il son origine aux artistes de notre pays, et doit il recevoir l'épithete de Français? N'est il autre chose qu'une imitation mal dirigée des monumens élevés par les Sarrasins en Espagne, et faut il appeler Sarrasin, ou Mauresque le style de nos constructions du 11, 12, et 13 siècle?

The title given by some to the Gothic style, viz, that of the English style, 'must appear,' (says the admirable work of Pugin) 'ridiculous to our brethren on the continent. Germany, France and Flanders possess Gothic churches, palaces, and towers, at least as magnificent as those of England, and of as early date. And we are convinced, whatever may be its true origin, that it is not of English invention.' 'The pointed arch,' says he elsewhere, 'may have been brought from the East.'

day brought home from Palestine all that had impressed them as most attractive and beautiful in the architecture of the East, adapted it to ecclesiastical purposes, and thus became designers of a style of building, previously, indeed, unknown in Europe, but for which they did not feel particularly anxious to acknowledge themselves indebted to the *paynim* of the Holy Land.

But if we suppose that such was the mode in which the Gothic style was introduced into Europe, a difficulty occurs in the name by which it has become generally known; for why should it be termed *Gothic* if its origin was in Palestine? In answer to this, it may be sufficient to state that this name is commonly agreed to be the product of the dislike entertained against it by the architects of the sixteenth century, who, being desirous to establish the Italian style, in their devotion to the works of Vitruvius and Palladio, called the eastern style *Gothic*, in order to express their opinion of its comparative barbarism.* All late writers seem to admit that this name is every way objectionable; and many other appellations have been suggested as more appropriate. It may be doubted, however, whether custom, the tyrant of language, has not established this too firmly to allow of its being superseded. But if another term could be generally agreed on, perhaps the Eastern style, or the Ecclesiastical style, would be preferable to most of the phrases recommended by writers on the subject.

Still the question recurs, what was the origin of this style? Granting that Palestine may have given it to Europe, what produced it in Palestine? In reply, it ought to be observed that the distinguishing features of this style are not confined to Palestine, but are diffused generally throughout the East. Thus, in India, the mausoleum of Sultan Chusero, and that of Sultan Purviez near Allahabad—the Jummah Musjed at Delhi—the Punj Mahalla Gate at Lucknow—the ruins at Cannonge—the gate of the mosque built by Hafiz Ramut at Pillibeat, and the interior of the palace, Madura,—all exhibit striking coincidences of forms, proportions, and details, with the style in question. At Constantinople† the mosques of Sultan Ah-

---

* 'A pedantic affectation of Italian taste' says Pugin, (1. vol. p. 10) had branded the pointed arch and all the buildings constructed on its principles, with the opprobrious term *Gothic*, an epithet inconsiderately applied, merely as designating something barbarous and devoid of regular design."

† See 'Tableau General de l'Empire Ottoman, par D'Ohisson.'

med, and of St. Sophia, and the sepulchral chapel of the Sultaness Valide, exhibit the buttress, the pointed arch, the lattice sash, the embattled top, the dome, the fret-work of the ceiling—all of the same character. Nay, in the mosque of St. Athanasius, at Alexandria, which cannot be later than the fourth century, we find, in the accurate drawing of Denon, the ogee pointed arch, the quatre foil, and the common pointed arch, together with the battlement, the buttress, the dome, and a lofty minaret, clearly proving that this style was then familiar. To these proofs we may add, that the public buildings of the Chinese * display in many important particulars, a close correspondence with the same style. Now when it is remembered that a peculiar species of architecture, and one, too, which demands great skill and labor in its execution, cannot spring up and reach perfection in a period less than many centuries—when we recollect especially, that the Eastern nations in general are noted for the wonderful constancy with which they retain their ancient dress, manners, and customs—a constancy incomparably greater than that of Europe—and when we call to mind the fact, that notwithstanding the disposition to innovate, the art of Architecture, in all other respects, is much the same that it was two thousand years ago, it will I think be sufficiently plain, that a style so prevalent in its principal features through all the vast regions of Asia, which were first settled after the flood, must in all probability have been invented long before the Grecian orders, since these were confessedly improved from the Egyptian architecture.†

---

* 'In both the antique and Chinese architecture' says Chambers, 'the general form of almost every composition has a tendency to the pyramidal figure—fret-work is likewise very frequent among the Chinese,—and (like the *Goths*) they always leave the timber work of the roof exposed within side, and often make both it and the columns which support it of precious wood, sometimes enriching them with ornaments.' &c.

In the plates belonging to Chambers' work on Chinese architecture, although they are neither various nor of the best selection for such a purpose, we may discover the Gothic forms of panel and fret-work, the foliage at the corners and the top of the roof, and the lofty towers, which are peculiar to the Eastern style, and are entirely foreign to the Greek and Roman architecture. The corroborations of our theory furnished by Chambers are altogether accidental on his part, for he seems to have had no taste nor knowledge on the subject of the Gothic style.

† Thus Dr. Shaw remarks (Travels, p. 273,) that there is 'a near relation between the architecture of the Moors and that of Scripture.'

But in my mind, there are traces of something like positive evidence in favor of this conclusion; for I think there are remarkable indications, at least, that the Temple of Solomon claimed affinity in many respects with what we now call the ecclesiastical Gothic style. And it may be well to state, somewhat in detail, the reasons for this opinion.

First, then, the proportions of the temple were of this character, viz.

Length, (counting twenty two inches to the cubit)	110 feet
Breadth,	36 "
Projection of the front porch,	18 "
Height of the main building,	55 "
Height of the porch or tower,	220 "

Excluding the space occupied by the Holy of Holies, which was 36 feet square, it was twice as long as it was broad, and twice as high as it was long, approximating closely in its three principal dimensions to the proportions generally adopted in the best cathedrals.

Secondly, it had chambers on the outside, three stories in height, each story being five cubits, making 27½ feet in the whole. Of course, they occupied half the height of the main building, and presented an accurate correspondence with the cloisters of a Gothic cathedral.

Thirdly, the temple had windows of *narrow lights*. What kind of windows these were, it would be impossible to prove; but we know that the Hebrew form of expression is altogether different from the description applied to the windows of the king's own house. We also know that the Gothic window is extremely narrow in proportion to its height; and further, we are certain that these windows of the temple must have been over the chambers of the priests, and thus that they admitted the light from above, which gives us another correspondence with the mode in which the nave of a Gothic cathedral receives its light from the windows over the roof of the cloisters.*

---

* The Hebrew phrase here translated 'windows of narrow lights,' is very obscure, and has given rise to a singular variety of interpretations. The original is חלני שקפים אטמים (1 Ki. 6. 5,) which Montanus translates '*fenestras prospectivas occlusas*,' and Taylor's Concordance agrees with this, while

Fourthly, we find that the cedar wood with which the temple was lined, was carved with 'knops and flowers,' and this gives us a very good description, in popular terms, of the rosettes, crocketts, and finials, which so profusely adorn the enriched, or florid Gothic style, and which form a regular part of the Turkish, Indian, and Chinese architecture.

Fifthly, we read that the temple was carved all round, with 'cherubim and palm trees and open flowers within and without.' Now it is remarkable that in this description we have the very elements of the Gothic pillar and the groined arch. For palm trees, with their lofty and slender trunks and branching heads, if placed in rows so that their boughs should interlace, would form the best imaginable prototype of the cathedral fretwork ceiling, springing from the heads of the pillars, and arching round in every direction. And the cherubim placed between, with open flowers, would seem to have suggested the idea of the statues of the ancient churches, under their canopies of tracery and foliage.

Sixthly, we read of two pillars ornamented with 'net-work, pomegranates, and lily work upon the top of the pillars;' which certainly bore no likeness to any thing we know of, unless it be the Gothic pinnacles which sometimes surmount the pillars, with their leafy ornaments; or the richly carved minarets of Asiatic architecture.

It appears deserving of much observation, in estimating the testimony of the Scriptures on this subject, that soon after the temple was completed, Solomon erected another building, with parts and proportions of the Egyptian, or what was subsequently refined into the Grecian style. I allude to 'the house of the forest

---

it also justifies the common version. The Septuagint has θυρίδας παρακυπτομένας; κρυπτάς. The Vulgate has '*fenestras obliquas:*' the German has ' Fenster inwendig weit, auswendig enge. ' The French agrees with it, calling them ' *Fenêtres à la maison, large en dedans, et étroites par dehors.* ' The Italian gives us '*finestre reticolate;*' the Spanish '*ventanas transversales;*' and Jahn, in his Archæologia Bib. in Comp. Red. § 338, says on the passage ' *Fenestræ erant decussatæ et clathris clausæ.* ' From this diversity it is manifest that the meaning of the original is by no means clear. It is sufficient for my purpose that the windows of the temple were peculiar in their form, and described in words altogether different from those of the king's palace.

of Lebanon,' perhaps so called from its multitude of cedar pillars. The dimensions of this building were as follows; viz.

Length,	183 feet
Breadth,	91 "
Height,	55 "

'It stood upon four rows of cedar pillars, with cedar beams upon the pillars, and it was covered with cedar above upon the beams, that lay on forty-five pillars, fifteen in a row, and there were windows in three rows, and light was against light, in three ranks. And he made a porch of pillars, the length thereof was 50 cubits,' (91¼ feet) &c. 1 Ki. 7 Ch. 2nd to 6th v.

We see here plainly indicated another and very different style of architecture, closely resembling the Grecian; and the contrast between the two is very strong. The temple is almost twice as high as it is broad, but the house of the forest of Lebanon, is almost twice as broad as it is high. The first has no pillars. The lofty palm trees fill the place which the slender Gothic pillars would now occupy. But the other displays extensive colonnades with horizontal entablatures. The first receives its light from above: the other has light against light in three ranks. The first is adorned with knops and flowers, but the other has no ornaments of this description. Hence we see Solomon executing two kinds of edifice of very different proportions and character: the one, sacred; the other, secular; both corresponding with considerable exactness to the two great styles of architecture which we behold at the present day. And if, indeed, this celebrated king was the founder of Balbec and Palmyra, as some have supposed, we need not be surprized at the Grecian taste of their ruins, when we recognize, in the description of the house of the forest of Lebanon, the very same features; and recollect that what Solomon began, others must have enlarged and improved at a subsequent period.

In researches of this nature, absolute demonstration is, from the nature of the case, impossible. The true origin of Architecture, like that of all other arts, lies buried in remote antiquity, and it is by no means improbable that it had reached a degree of perfection even before the flood, of which we have no idea. Cain, we know, built a city. Tubal Cain was an artificer in brass and iron; and what progress might not have been expected in knowledge as well as vice, when the age of man averaged eight hundred years! But of the extent of these primæval acquisitions, we know nothing. Nor, at a period long subsequent, are we able to ascertain the details of taste which characterised the magnificence of ancient Nineveh and Babylon. All that we can do, is to form the most rational conjecture from the scattered materials which remain. While, therefore, we have the most distinct evidence for the antiquity of both the Gothic and the Grecian styles, if not in all their minutiæ, yet in their leading peculiarities—while we see the Asiatic nations, which are undoubtedly the oldest, universally employing the characteristics of the Gothic style; and the whole posterity of Shem exhibiting the same general affinity in this, as in their language, their dress, and their social habits—while, above all, we see considerable points of correspondence with this style in the temple of Solomon—we cannot err in assuming it as highly *probable*, at least, that the style in question is the most ancient in the world which has been applied to sacred purposes; and that it deserves to be esteemed, not only for its solemn beauty, and its general fitness for the offices of religion, but for its special application to those very objects by the chosen people of God.

CHAPTER II.

ON THE EXPENSE REQUIRED FOR THIS STYLE OF ARCHITECTURE.

It is the opinion of some very judicious writers, that the Gothic, or Eastern style, is only fit for large buildings, where it can be carried out in full perfection. But I doubt the correctness of this idea. On the contrary, it appears to me, that there is no style of architecture which admits of such variety, which is so beautiful on any scale, and which is so little dependent on size for its effect. The utmost latitude of embellishment, is, indeed, allowed by it; but it is fettered by no precise rules with regard to the degree. And although the kind of ornament and finish is fixed by examples, from which no man of judgment or good taste would venture to depart; yet the distinctive characters of the style may be preserved in union with the utmost simplicity. The general proportion, securing a due height in all its dimensions—buttresses, producing strong perpendicular lines of light and shade, and terminating in pinnacles—battlements, breaking the horizontal line, where it is next the sky—pointed arches, enclosing at least two subdivisions in the windows; and both windows and doors retreating from the outside of the walls, so as to furnish strong shadows, and increase the solemnity of the effect—these seem to present the prominent external features of the style, and may be preserved in connexion with the highest ornament, or with none at all, just as circumstances may require. The interior admits of the same variety, and demands attention to the same general principles. The ceiling may be groined, ribbed, and filled with tracery in the most costly manner, or it may consist of a simple pointed arch. It may be supported on clusters of slender pillars, or it may spring from the walls in the plainest form. But its terminating line should never be horizontal. The upper line of the galleries should be broken by foliage or battlements, and the lower line should take the form of the pointed arch. All the panel work should give preponderance to the effect of the perpendicular line, and every termination which admits of it, should come to a point. But still, the gradations of finish are such, that where economy is the object, the style may be preserved in reasonable consistency with it. Proportions and forms must be marked, but ornament, in which the expense is chiefly involved, is arbitrary; and may be added afterwards, when the circumstances of those concerned shall allow.

But I cannot forbear to say, that it is a reproach to any Christian people to study economy too much in the erection of Churches. The Church is the house of God. It is the place where his people assemble to transact the concerns of eternity, and it is a disgrace to our professions of zeal in behalf of religion, when the private dwellings of the worshippers, exceed the temples of the Most High, in beauty and costliness of workmanship. The principle runs throughout the whole Bible, and is in accordance with right reason, that we should dedicate nothing to God, which is not the best of its kind in our power to procure; and although it is very true that the unhappy state of division which deforms the Christian world puts it out of our power to equal the magnificent erections of other days, yet the average standard of our efforts in this respect might be raised vastly above its present height, if Christians would learn to come up to the scriptural rule of 'honoring the Lord with their substance and with the first fruits of all their increase,' and remember that no rule of liberality is so likely to be acceptable in His sight as that which he himself enjoined upon ancient Israel.* True, the spi-

---

*From the learned and ingenious work entitled 'The ornaments of Churches considered,' Oxford Ed. of 1761, I extract the following just and eloquent argument of the famous Mede on this subject, which the scholar, the man of taste, and the divine, will read with pleasure.

'De Templorum magnificentia dicturus, ut caveam quæ in hac causa multi in hanc vel illam ornatus speciem importuni objiciunt, non simpliciter sed comparatè definio de modo et mensura ornatus sacri, nempe Dei domum esse debere æque, imo magis quam profana magnificam. In urbe Templum ædificas? pulcherrimum id sit omnium in urbe palatiorum. In villa? æquet imo vincat reliquas in villa ædes. Ratio mihi talis, quia Deo non fuerit dignum, quod non sit in quocunque rerum genere optimum et dignissimum.' 'There are two other objections to the decoration of Churchritual Church, composed of the living stones of the faithful, is the abiding temple which the Lord has promised to inhabit, and 'he dwelleth not in temples made with hands.' But although the wise king of Israel uttered this very sentiment in the dedication of the temple at Jerusalem, yet he made that house 'exceedingly magnifical,' and for an obvious reason; because it was a symbol of the heavenly temple where the redeemed should one day be privileged to worship with celestial joy. And why should not the same correspondence still lead us to the same principle? As the Sabbath of God is the most precious day to the Christian—as on that day he clothes his body in his best attire that it may answer to the clothing of the soul—Why should not the house of God be the most precious of all earthly edifices, and why should not every thing about it answer to the sublime and glorious end for which it was erected—the congregating together on earth, those who desire to worship him together in heaven?

---

es,' observes the author of the work above mentioned, 'one of which is taken notice of by Mede in the following words: 'At magnam nobis invidiam conflatum eunt de pauperum indigentia, indignum enim esse, ut auro splendescant templa hæc externa, dum viva Spiritûs Sancti habitacula fame contabescant et inediâ, in pauperes ut simus lapides, nimium in lapides profusi.' His answer to this is spirited to a great degree. 'Sciant non Templa sola hoc quod intorquent ariete, sed et regum conquassari palatia, sed multas privatorum ædes. Pauperes egent? Quin igitur tu aedes tuas dirue, quin regum et nobiliorum demolire. Pauperes egent? Quid tibi tantus domi aulæorum et tapetum apparatus? Quid tot contignationum et concamerationum deliciae? Quid reliqua supellex otiosa, ornatus supervacuus? Aufer, aufer haec, inquam, sine quibus et tibi satis erit domi et pauperi inde multum eleemosynae.'

'The other objection is drawn from the tendency which ornaments have to introduce superstition and popery. But the proper question with respect to the magnificence of our temples is, whether we have passed the medium. 'What,' says the great Chillingworth, 'if out of devotion to God, out of a desire that he should be worshipped as in spirit and in truth in the first place, so also in the beauty of holiness? What if out of fear that too much simplicity and nakedness in the public service of God, may beget in the ordinary sort of men, a dull and stupid irreverence, and out of hope that the outward state and glory of it, being well disposed and wisely moderated, may engender, quicken, increase and nourish, the inward respect and devotion which is due unto God's sovereign majesty and power? I say, what if out of these considerations, the governors of our Church, more of late than formerly, have set themselves to adorn and beautify the places, where God's honor dwells, and to make them as heavenlike as they can with earthly ornaments? Is this a sign that they are warping towards popery? Is this devotion in the Church of England, an argument that she is coming over to the Church of Rome?'

CHAPTER III.

ON THE DEGREE OF LIGHT EXPEDIENT IN CHURCHES.

There is no fault more common, and none more opposed by every principle of good taste, than the having too many windows in Churches. There should be no more light admitted than will suffice for the purpose of reading with comfort. More than this increases the expense, exposes to cold, and, above all,—so far as the eye is concerned,—destroys solemnity, and is unfriendly to devotion. Thus H. Wotton, in his elements of architecture, p. 35, asserts, that 'Light can misbecome no edifice whatever, temples only excepted, which were anciently dark; as they are likewise at this day in some proportion; devotion more requiring collected than diffused spirits.' And Sir Thomas More, describing the temples of his Utopia, says that they were somewhat obscure; not on account of the unskilfulness of the architects, but by the choice of the priesthood: because immoderate light scatters the thoughts.' *

The custom of staining the glass of Church windows, was admirably adapted not only to moderate the glare of light, but also to give it a rich, mellow, and solemn effect. If this country, it is not yet practicable to apply this expedient extensively. Instead of it, however, a very beautiful effect may be produced at a small expense, by transparencies painted on linen or muslin, in the Gothic style, and fixed inside the windows.

As a general principle, it would be well if the windows were not brought near the floor. A congregation assembled for worship have nothing to do with looking out, and the light has always the best effect when it enters the building as near to the top as possible, consistently with true proportion.

---

* 'Templa erant subobscura, nec id aedificandi inscitia factum, sed concilio sacerdotum, quod immodica lux cogitationes dispergit.'

CHAPTER IV.

ON MONUMENTS, CENOTAPHS, STATUES AND PICTURES, IN CHURCHES.

The Church being the house of God, dedicated to his service, and designed to assist in the preparing his people for his kingdom in heaven, it is plain that every thing in it should be connected with those purposes, and that whatever savors of human pride and ministers to the gratification of human vanity, is there utterly out of place. Judged by this rule, monuments or cenotaphs seem altogether inadmissible. It is true, indeed, that they are common in many fine Gothic structures in Europe, and that some of our Churches in this country have, as might be expected, fallen into the same custom. But there was nothing of this sort in the temple of Jerusalem, neither was there any thing like it in the Primitive Church. The early Christians did undoubtedly hold their worship in cemeteries, during the times of persecution; and at a somewhat later day they were fond of building Churches over the tombs of eminent saints; but it was long afterwards, and in a very dark and barbarous period, when the monuments of kings, and lords, and barons, were privileged with a place within the walls of the sanctuary.

What renders this thing, in my mind, the more unbecoming, is the indisputable fact, that the distinction thus granted is a boon conceded to rank, or wealth, and not to piety. So far, indeed, is religion from having any thing to do with it, that there are instances—not a few—where the Churches of the God of Holiness contain a standing commemoration of men whose lives would have scandalized, and whose deaths would have disgraced, a Christian profession. And shall the pride of surviving friends be gratified, by putting the lofty memorials of the sculptor's art upon the very walls of the sanctuary, in favor of such men as these? Surely it is enough if the church yard is left free for the pageantry of this poor ambition, without having the very enclosure consecrated to the Most High, profaned by these shrines of vanity and ostentation.

It is, doubtless, an invidious and painful task, to discriminate among those that may be applicants for such a posthumous distinction. The better and the safer rule therefore, would be this: That no man, whatever, shou'd have any such memorial in the house of God, unless he had already a place on the Church's calendar. This principle would prevent all difficulty, since an honor which the clergy disclaimed for themselves, could not and would not be expected by their people.

Pictures and statuary representing the characters and events recorded in the Scriptures, stand, of course, on a very different foundation. It is the design of the Lord that these characters and events should be commemorated in the Churches, and to that end, the reading of the Bible is an established part of our duty in his temple. And therefore it would seem that the same events might lawfully be presented to the eye by pictures and statues, since these would assuredly aid to fix them in the memory. Besides which general argument, it is to be remembered, that statues of cherubim were sculptured all round the temple of Jerusalem, and that the veil was covered with embroidery. Still it is very certain, that one of the early Councils of the Church expressly forbade pictures in Churches—that statuary, when first introduced, was warmly and violently opposed—that the case of ancient Israel was confined to the depicting of the cherubim, and that in neither temple nor synagogue was there any thing else that could be called picture or statue. Equally certain is it, that the custom, when finally established, led the way to a species of idolatry, at least, amongst the ignorant and superstitious; and that it is a kind of ornament, which, in its own nature, is liable to abuse. On the whole, therefore, I should recommend the adorning the walls of Churches only with the appropriate architectural enrichments, and with judicious and edifying selections from the word of God. These last cannot be too abundant, and should be so disposed, that the wandering eye might be arrested, on every side of the sacred edifice, by some counsel or warning of Divine truth, calculated to enlighten the conscience and amend the heart.

CHAPTER V.

ON THE PEWS OF CHURCHES.

Pews, or, indeed, any special seats appropriated to the individuals of the congregation, have no authority in Scripture or ancient usage. 'Before the age of the Reformation,' says Burns, (Eccl. Law, vol. 1. p. 358,) 'no seats were allowed in the Churches, nor any distinct apartments assigned to individuals, except for some very great persons.' And Pugin remarks, (p. 42) that 'the fastidious habits of modern times have sadly disfigured the interior of our Churches by the introduction of close pews. Instead of being shut up in square boxes, the congregation, formerly, were seated on long benches, ranged on each side the nave of the Church, with their faces turned towards the altar. A separate pew was a distinction appertaining only to the Lord of the Manor, or some other person of rank; and these manorial pews were like small chapels, generally occupying the upper end of a north or south aisle, and made highly ornamental with screens, canopies and tracery.'

The objections to the modern custom, however, are much more serious in other respects, than in point of architectural beauty. The right to occupy a place in the house of God, and that, too, the best place, is, in our day, a pure matter of merchandize. It is a right sold at auction, to the highest bidder. Religion has nothing to do with it. Personal piety has nothing to do with it. The seats next to the altar, and in the immediate eye of the ministers of Christ, may be occupied by men who have no real respect for the Gospel or its ordinances, and who exhibit, in the gaze of the whole congregation, a constant example of ungodliness. Still, they pay for their seats, and the omnipotence of gold covers the glaring inconsistency. And while every desirable place in a fashionable Church is thus appropriated to a special owner, the poor man—though pious and sincere, and longing to have his portion of the bread of life—is afraid to come forward in the midst of so much exclusive pride : and either takes his seat afar off, or goes away to some humbler assembly, where he can worship on a level with his fellow creatures, before that God who is no respecter of persons.

Neither is this the whole of the evil. Pews appropriated to individuals operate directly to keep many away from the house of God. Strangers do not like to intrude on other persons' property, nor to run the risk of being turned out of their seat by the owner. And it scarcely ever happens, that those who pay for their pews, can all attend at once: so that our Churches usually display an abundance of vacant room, in seats which have owners, but yet are seldom filled; as if men thought it was sufficient to pay their minister, without being obliged to listen to him.

The luxurious accommodations of particular pews produce another variety of the same evil; for even when strangers are determined to meet the risk of being turned out of their places, it is by no means pleasant to use the silken couches, and tread the rich carpets, and open the splendid prayer books, prepared for the sons and daughters of opulence and fashion; when the intruder is conscious, that if the owners were present, they would probably give him the cold look of unwilling sufferance.

But worst of all, is a method of constructing the pews, which has become very common, and which looks as if it had been contrived by some enemy to the work of devotion. We refer to the making them so narrow, that kneeling is impossible; and all that the worshippers can do is to adopt a compound posture, half sitting and half kneeling, which usually ends in sitting altogether. And a foul reproach it surely is, that a Church which boasts of her liturgy, and in this very point of kneeling in prayer, claims a superiority over other portions of the Christian family, should have slidden into a practice, within one generation, which is not only in direct contradiction to her own formularies, and to the authority of Scripture, but which must inevitably tend to prevent the Divine blessing on the worship of her people.

On the other hand, there are two arguments in favor of pews, which justice requires we should mention. The first is, that they afford *families* a better opportunity to worship together; and the second is, that they facilitate the collection of the Church revenue.

We grant both these positions, although we think them by no means of sufficient force to justify the custom. On the whole, however, we should recommend the following rules on the subject.

The old mode of benches, would be best. They should be substantial, made in Gothic style, to correspond with the building, and should have backs, for the comfort of the aged or infirm. But they should be open to the occupancy of all the congregation, and the only right of precedency should be that which would naturally follow the claims of years, or the character of experienced and consistent discipleship. Those who had children to watch over, might take their place a little earlier; but no children should be carried to the house of public worship so young, as to trouble and interrupt the devotions of others. It is obvious that on this plan the revenues of the Church could not be charged upon the seats, but they could be collected, as they now are for all other purposes, by voluntary subscription.

But if pews must be retained, in compliance with the present custom, they should be made at least three feet wide, to allow abundant room for kneeling; and they should never be furnished in a style beyond what reasonable comfort and moderation would justify. The house of God is no place for the display of vanity or ostentation; and there, at least, if no where else, men should learn to feel, that however they may differ in their worldly circumstances, they are nevertheless equal, by the rights of nature and of grace; and that the superiority of their earthly rank can avail them nothing before the final tribunal. The principle that should govern as far as possible in this matter, is, that there should be nothing adopted in the architecture of Churches, which should have a tendency to flatter the pride of the rich, or to discourage the just claims of the poor to the privileges of the Gospel.

CHAPTER VI.

ON THE COLORS APPROPRIATE TO THE GOTHIC STYLE.

SOLEMNITY and repose, being the characteristics of this mode of architecture, every thing light and gaudy should be excluded. The only contradiction which might seem to oppose this rule is found in the windows, which we have recommended to be either of stained glass, or covered with transparencies in imitation of it. But this is an exception strictly proper, not only because the light admitted through such a medium is in reality much softened and subdued, but also because the crimson and gold and blue, in the midst of which the light of nature—the sun in the firmament—is presented to the eye by the munificent hand of the Creator, seem to afford an analogy which justifies us in connecting the same hues with the light transmitted into the house of God.

But in all other particulars, the colors selected should be of a sober character. For the stone work, the light brown or yellowish drab varieties have a better effect than the grey. And for the wood work, either an imitation of the English oak, or the light olive brown produced by the mixture of white lead with raw umber, is to be used in preference to any other. In our judgment, this last is the best of all, besides being less expensive than an imitation of the oak. Blue, grey, and lead color, have a cold and chilling appearance which forbids their use, excepting in the sashes of the windows; but the raw umber mixed with white (when the umber is of a good quality) gives a great variety of shades, from light drab color to a dark brown, by a judicious employment of which, great richness and harmony of effect can be secured in union with solemnity. For inscriptions on the walls, it is best to make the body of the letters considerably lighter than the ground, and shade them with a tint nearly as dark as the pure umber, which gives them the appearance of being raised, and looks, to our taste, better than gilding.

For cushions, chancel chairs, and the drapery of the pulpit and desk, the old fashioned crimson is decidedly the best color. The purple which has been employed of late instead of it, looks very well in a strong light; but when the day is cloudy, or by lamp light, it cannot be distinguished from black, and reminds the spectator of clothing the Church in mourning. Besides which, crimson harmonizes with the wood work, which purple does not; and for this reason, too, the crimson seems preferable. It is to be observed, however, by those who are not much skilled in colors, that while crimson is appropriate, bright red or scarlet is altogether inadmissible.

The ancient mode of making the sash which contained the glass of Church windows, was in lattice work of lead or pewter. Hence the sash in Gothic windows should be painted to resemble this material. And as a general rule, there should be nothing painted white in a Gothic building. The lightest tint should be a shade of drab color. This does not seem a very desirable hue for any thing, according to the common judgment; but being in fact a stone color, it forms the most sober and pleasing finish, for the inside walls and wood work of a Church. It is solemn without being gloomy, and shews the workmanship of every part to the best advantage.

These are *little things*, and we should not mention them if it were not for the instances we have seen, where mistakes in them had spoiled the whole effect of an otherwise fine building.

CHAPTER VII.

ON THE CEILINGS OF CHURCHES.

The most beautiful mode of constructing the ceilings of large Churches, is in groined arches, the rules for which are the same in this, that they are in the Roman style; the only difference being, that the arch in Gothic architecture must always be pointed in the centre, instead of being a regular segment of a circle. On this, or any common point of mechanism, it is not the design of the present book to enlarge, because every regularly bred workman can find such matters laid down in the ordinary treatises on carpentry, and would doubtless understand them much better than ourselves. We would only remark, that for small Churches, a flat ceiling would probably be preferable to any arch whatever, on account of the echo produced by the arch whenever the ceiling is not very high, and which is a serious obstacle to the distinctness of the preacher's voice. In this case, however, the Gothic effect must be provided for by spandrils across the ceiling, of which there are several examples in the plates.

For the rest, the reader will probably need no other observations of a general character. The plates, together with the explanations and dimensions attached to them, will be his best directory; and to these we will now refer him, only premising a brief history of the Gothic style in England, and a Glossary of the technical terms used in this kind of architecture.

CHAPTER VIII.

A CHRONOLOGICAL SKETCH OF ENGLISH ARCHITECTURE, EXTRACTED FROM THE WORK OF PUGIN.

1. The Anglo-Saxon, or Saxon style, from A. D. 597, to A. D. 1066.

THE buildings erected in England during the four centuries preceding the Norman conquest, have usually been designated Anglo-Saxon, or Saxon; but as there is no positive proof that we have any examples extant of this style, it can only be conjectured to have been a modification of Roman architecture.

2. Anglo-Norman or Norman style, from A. D. 1066, to A. D. 1189.

The Normans rebuilt almost every eminent Church during this period, and a prodigious number of castles. The style of these buildings is distinguished by strong and ponderous dimensions, round arches, and various mouldings peculiar to itself. This style resulted from sundry modifications of the Roman, and it has been very properly contended that it ought to be called the *Romanesque.*

3. From A. D. 1189, to A. D. 1272.

The general adoption of the pointed arch, and a change from broad and massy forms to tall and slender proportions, were fully established in the reign of King John, but had appeared a few years earlier in two or three instances. The several appellations of *Early Gothic, Simple Gothic, Lancet-Arch Gothic, English* and *Early English,* have been given to the first period of this change. The most complete specimen of it is Salisbury Cathedral, and it may be considered as extending through the reigns of Richard 1, John, and Henry 3.

4. From A. D. 1272, to 1377.

The 13th century was not closed before the simple style of Salisbury Cathedral became superseded by one of a richer character. Westminster Abbey is perhaps the earliest example on a large scale. Lincoln Cathedral in its eastern part, is a richer specimen. About the middle of the 14th century a new fashion of tracery in the heads of windows became apparent, wherein the curves were blended like the fibres of a leaf. Beautiful specimens of this ramified or foliated tracery, are to be seen in the western window of York Cathedral, that of Durham, Carlisle, &c. This has been termed *pure Gothic, absolute Gothic, decorated English, &c.*

5. From A. D. 1377 to A. D. 1460.

The lofty and simple form of the pointed arch, when struck from two centres on the line of its base, began to be given up for a lower and more complicated form, in the reign of Richard, 2. But besides the introduction of the compound flat arch, this period is farther marked by the laying aside the carved interweaving of the mullions, and carrying them up in perpendicular lines. This style has been called *ornamented Gothic, perpendicular English,* &c.

6. From A. D. 1460, to A. D. 1547.

The last period of the Gothic style is marked by the general use of the flat or compound pointed arch. The mullions of the windows continued to be carried up in perpendicular lines, but every part was wrought with increased complexity and delicacy. King's College Chapel, Cambridge, St. George's, Windsor, and Henry the Seventh's Chapel at Westminster, are the grandest examples of this style, which has been designated *Florid Gothic, Florid English,* &c.

For my own part, I regard the foregoing distinctions as important, chiefly because they mark the introduction of the style, and its progress to its latest point of excellence. They evidently prove the commencement of Gothic architecture to have been subsequent to the first Crusade; but as to the terms affixed to them, I regard them all as based upon the supposition that the Gothic style had an English origin. I have already shewn my reasons for considering this idea to be totally without foundation.

CHAPTER IX.

A GLOSSARY OF TECHNICAL TERMS IN GOTHIC ARCHITECTURE, EXTRACTED FROM PUGIN'S SPECIMENS. Vol. 1.*

AILE, (*ala ecclesiæ*, Lat. *L'aile de l'eglise*, Fr.) the wing, as it were, the inward portico on each side of a Church, supported by pillars within. Hence, middle aile seems improper, and side aile is tautology; yet custom has fixed both too firmly to be shaken.

ALLEY, (*allée*, Fr.) an aîle, any part of a Church left open for walking through. Hence in some old surveys of Cathedrals these terms occur, 'the Dean's alley, the chanter's alley, the cross alley.'

ARCH-BUTTRESS, (*arc boutant*, Fr.) an arch springing over the roof of an aile or cloister, and abutting against the wall of a clere-story. It is also called a Flying buttress, and it is applied to the sides of spires, lanterns, &c.

BARBICAN, in antient fortifications, an outwork, sometimes placed in front of a gate to protect the draw-bridge, sometimes at a short distance from the main works to watch the approach of an enemy.

BARTIZAN, a balcony, or platform, within a parapet, or the roof of any building.

BASE-COURT, (*Basse-cour*, Fr.) a yard attached to a castle or large mansion, around which the culinary and other offices were built.

BASTILE, a tower, or bulwark in the fortification of a town.

---

* It may be proper to observe that the literary part of Pugin's excellent work is by EDWARD JAMES WILLSON. I have inserted in this Glossary, many terms which do not come within the strict design of my humble performance, but which it will be interesting and useful to the general reader, to have explained.

BATTLEMENT, a parapet on the roof of a building, cut into loops or embrasures to shoot through.

BAY, 1. an opening: 2. an arbitrary measure of size in a building: 3. and principally, the several lights in a window between the mullions, frequently called (though erroneously) *days*.

BAY-WINDOWS, an oriel, or projecting window. Sometimes improperly called a *bow window*.

BELFRY, a tower for bells.

BOTTEL, 1. the perpendicular shafts of a clustered column. 2. Such shafts attached to the jambs of windows or doors. 3. Any round moulding. It is the old English term for the *torus* of the Italian architects.

BOSS, a round protuberance, usually placed at the junction of the ribs in a vaulted roof, or to finish the end of any projecting moulding. These were variously carved.

BRACKETT, (*brachium*, Lat.) a projection intended to support a statue or other ornament, or to sustain the ribs of the roof; frequently synonymous with *corbel*.

BUTTRESS, a pillar built against the wall to strengthen it.

CANTED, (adj.) of a polygonal plan, as, a canted window or oriel.

CAROL or CARREL, a little pew or closet in a cloister to sit and read in; so called from the *carols*, or sentences inscribed on the walls.—(Qu. Is it not more probably derived from *Quarré*, the French for square.)

CASEMENT, 1. a light or compartment, within the mullions of a window; or 2. and chiefly, a frame enclosing part of the glazing of a window, with hinges to open and shut.

CHAMFER, the angle of the jamb of a door or of an arch, &c. canted, or cut off diagonally.

CHEVERON, see *Zigzag*.

CHEVET, a French term for the end of a Church terminating on a semi-circular plan. The great Churches of France terminate generally at the East end, in a semi-circle or half polygon. This end is called the *chevet*.

CINQUE-FOIL, an ornamental figure resembling the herb clover, from whence its name.

CLERE-STORY, the upper story of a tower, Church, or other building.

COIN, or QUOIN, the outward corner of a building.

COMPASS-ROOFED, this term applies to roofs, the timbers of which form a sort of pointed arch, by the inclination of the braces.

COMPASS WINDOW, a bay window, or oriel.

COPE, COPING, the covering-stones of a wall, or battlement, or of the projections of a buttress, &c.

CORBEL, CORBET, or CORBETEL, a bracket; a projection from a wall or buttress, to support an image; or the springing of an arch, &c.

CORBIE-STEPS, battlements rising like steps on the sides of gables, so called because the crows (*corbeau*) were observed to perch upon them.

CORBEL-TABLE, a projecting battlement, parapet, or cornice, resting on corbels.

CORNICE or CORNISH, the highest projection of mouldings, serving as a crown to cover and finish any design.

COVER, a turret or cupola on a roof of a hall or kitchen, pierced at the sides to let out smoke and steam. See *Louvre*.

CRENELLE, the opening of a battlement, an embrasure.

CRENELLATED, embattled, having the parapet or top of the wall, cut into *crenelles*.

CREST, an imagery or carved work, to adorn the head or top of any thing.

CREST-TILE, ridge tiles to cover the top of a roof, which anciently were often curiously moulded into the form of little battlements or leaves.

CROCKET, CROCHET, CROTCHET, (*crochet*, Fr.) the projecting parts of the foliage running up arches, pinnacles, &c. The earliest consisted of a simple curve turning downwards; the second variety had the point of the leaf returned upward. The diversity of foliage carved on crockets is very great: and in a few of the latest buildings of the 15th century, animals were sculptured creeping on the angles, in place of crockets.

CUSP, a modern term for those segments of circles placed in compartments to form trefoils, quatrefoils, or other tracery.

DAIS, the plat form or raised floor at the upper end of antient dining halls, where the high table stood. Also, a seat with a high back and a canopy, for guests of rank.

DANCETTE, a term applied to the ancient *Norman zigzag* moulding.

DAY, the same as *Bay;* the light of a mullioned window.

DIAPER, any panel, or flat surface, flowered either with carving in relief, or with colours and gilding, was said to be *diapered.*

DORMANT or DORMER WINDOW, a window set upon the sloping side of a roof.

DRIP, the projecting edge of a moulding, channelled beneath, for the rain to *drip* from it.

DONGEON, the chief tower of a castle: the *Keep.*

EMBRASURE, see *Crenelle.*

ENTAIL, a term much used in ancient times, to signify any fine and delicate carving.

ENTERCLOSE, a passage connecting two rooms.

ENTER-SOLE, a story of small rooms betwixt two floors of larger ones.

FALSE-ROOF, the open space between the ceiling and the rafters.

FANE or VANE, a plate of metal turning on a spindle at the top of a tower or pinnacle, to show the course of the wind.

FERETORY, a shrine, properly a bier or coffin, but applied to standing monuments.

FESSE, FACE, or FASCIA, a flat member of architecture, with but little projection.

FILLET, a narrow, flat moulding; also called *list* or *annulet.*

FINIAL, the top or finishing of a pinnacle or gable, as it is now generally understood; but antiently an entire pinnacle was sometimes described by this term.

FOOT-PACE, see *Dais.*

FOOT-STALL, the plinth, or base of a pillar.

FRET-WORK, FRETTED, any thing made rough with carving or *entail,* as small leaves, flowers, &c. applied to ceilings, doors, &c.

GABLE, or GAVEL, the pyramidal wall which covers the end of a roof. It is also extended in signification to the whole end wall of a building.

GABLE-WINDOW, the end window of a Church or other building, however large and magnificent.

GABLET, a little gable, a common ornament for tabernacles, screens, &c. Previous to the 14th century these resembled the real gable of a roof. Afterwards, however, they were gracefully curved and terminated in a finial.

GARGLE or GARGYLE, the figure of a serpent or monster, with the mouth pierced, for the water spout of a roof, or a fountain to run through.

GARLAND, a band of ornamental work, surrounding the top of a spire, tower, &c.

GENTESE, see *Cusp*.

GREES, steps, or stairs.

GROIN, the intersection of two vaulted roofs, crossing each other. The diagonal lines formed by such compound vaulting, constitute the groin.

HERSE, or HEARSE, a frame set over a coffin, and covered with a pall. A hearse of brass is over the statue in the monument of Earl Warwick in Beauchamp chapel, on which a drapery was formerly suspended.

HOOD-MOULD, the outer moulding over the head of a door, window, or other opening, so called because it covers the other mouldings within. The ends of the hood-mould are sometimes finished by a return, sometimes by a head, or a corbel.

HOUSES, or HOUSINGS, niches for statues.

HOVEL, the canopy over the head of a statue.

JUBE, A gallery with a sort of pulpit attached to the front, carried over the entrance into the choir of a Cathedral, for the reader of the lessons.

KEEP, see *Dongeon*.

KERNEL, the same as *Crenelle*. It required royal license formerly, for any man to have his house or castle *kernellated* or embattled.

KNOB, KNOPPE, see *Boss*. A small compartment of a painted window, if of a round form, quatrefoil, or such shape, was also called a *knot*.

LABEL, the same as *Hood-mould*, which see.

LANTERN, a turret or cupola: see *Cover*. Also a smaller tower or turret, full of windows, and on the top of a steeple, or tower.

LATTEN, LATTIN, or LATEN, brass.

LECTERN, or LETTERN, a desk for a large book to lie on.

LIGHT, each distinct opening of a mullioned window.

LOOP or LOOP-HOLE, a narrow window to light a stair case or closet. Also the *crenelle* or *embrasure* of a battlement.

LOUVRE, the same as *Cover*.

LUCAINE, a window set upon the sloping side of a roof: a garret window. See *Dormant.*

MACHECOULIS, or MASCHECOULIS, commonly called *macchicolations.* Grooves or openings within the parapet of a fortified tower, for the purpose of throwing down stones, molten lead, hot sand, or boiling water, upon the heads of assailants, or to shoot down upon them unseen.

MANTLE TREE, a beam laid across the opening of a large fire-place.

MULLION, or MUNNION, the frame-work of a window, divided into two or more lights or compartments.

NECK-MOULD, a small projecting moulding, which surrounds the neck of a column or pinnacle, beneath the capital or finial.

NOSING, the projecting edge of a moulding. See *Drip.*

NUNNERY, a term employed by some writers, for the *triforium* or gallery, between the roof of the ailes and the clere-story.

OEILLET, EYLET, or OYLET, a loop-hole; a small window.

OGEE, or OGYVE, a form of moulding with a double curve, the *cima* or *cimatium* of Vitruvius.

ORIEL, or ORYEL, a bay window or compass window: sometimes applied to signify recesses, or closets, or a *boudoir.*

PANE, the light of a mullioned window: the pieces of glass in it: the side of a spire or tower, or of a cloister.

PANEL, a compartment enclosed with mouldings. The same, sometimes, as *Pane.*

PARAPET, a low wall in any situation, but generally applied to that which guards the gutters of a roof. If a parapet is cut into embrasures, it is called a *battlement.*

PARVIS, a porch, or court of entrance to a great Church, or palace.

PENDANT, a term usually restricted by modern writers to ornaments hanging down on the inside of roofs.

PERCH, PERK, PEARCH, see *Brackett* and *Corbel.*

PINNACLE, a turret: a spire: any tall perpendicular ornament.

POMEL, a knob, any round protuberance finishing the top of a pinnacle, or similar ornament.

Poop, the high ends of the seats in the antient Churches, with *finials* or crests carved on their tops.

Presbytery, the eastern parts of large Churches, kept exclusively for the use of the clergy.

Purfled, trimmed with knots, crockets, or flourishings at the edges.

Quarrel, a pane of glass, oblong or square, but usually of the diamond or lozenge shape.

Quarter, a square panel.

Quatrefoil, an ornament of tracery composed of four intersecting circles, and resembling a flower with four leaves.

Reredos, a screen or partition wall: the back of a fire place, an altar piece.

Respond, or responder, a half column or pilaster attached to a wall, and *responding* to another, or to a pillar opposite to it.

Rood-loft, a gallery over the entrance into the choir of the greater Churches, so called from the *Rood* or cross, which stood in front. Since the Reformation the Rood lofts have become Organ lofts.

Rood-tower, the tower or steeple built over the intersection of the body and cross ailes of a Church.

Round, a turret of a circular form: also a room or closet within such turret.

Rose-window, a circular window, sometimes called a Catharine wheel window, from the resemblance of such windows to a wheel in the form of their mullions.

Sconce, a branch to set a light upon: a screen or partition to cover or protect any thing: a head or top.

Scutcheon, a shield of arms: also a quoin or angle buttress.

Shaft, a *bottel*, or slender perpendicular part of a clustered column.

Shrine, a case wherein the remains of saints were preserved.

Spandril, applied to the arches formed within a square of a ceiling, door, or other opening: the open (or ornamented) space between the outward moulding of an arch, from its impost to the horizontal line which surmounts it above.

STALL, a seat for an ecclesiastic in the choir or chancel of a Church. Every stall was enclosed for a single person only to sit in.

STANCHEON, the upright iron bars of a window.

STOUP, a post, or small pedestal for a statue.

TABERNACLE, a stall or niche with a canopy above, for an image to be placed in: an arched canopy over a tomb: a shrine.

TRACERY, a term much used by modern writers for the ornamental pattern formed by the tracing or interweaving of the mullions in a window, or the fret-work in a roof.

TRANSEPT, a cross aisle.

TREFOIL, an ornament resembling the three-leaved clover.

TRELLICE, a gate or screen of open work, whether wood or metal.

TURN-PIKE, a flight of stairs winding round a centre.

VICE, a spiral stair case; the same as the foregoing.

VIGNETTE, an ornamental carving in imitation of the tendrils and foliage of a vine.

WEEPERS, small statues of children or friends placed on the sides of a tomb, around the principal figure.

ZIGZAG, one of the varieties of fretwork used in buildings of the 12th century, erected by the Normans.

EXPLANATION OF THE PLATES.

PLATE I.

THE upper half of this plate presents various modes of forming Gothic arches, copied from 'Pugin's Specimens,' and selected from several edifices in England.

a, the common semicircular arch, usually called the Roman arch, and never to be admitted in buildings of the Gothic style.

b, the four-centred pointed arch. The dots shew the place of the compasses in describing this arch.

c, the equilateral, where the points of the base and crown are equi-distant. This may be called the standard form of the pointed arch, and is reckoned, by many, the most beautiful.

d, the lancet arch, described from two centres outside the arch.

e, the three-centred pointed arch.

f, the four-centred pointed arch in another form.

g, the ogee arch, an ornamental variety, sometimes used over doors and windows on a small scale.

h, the four-centred ogee arch.

i & j, other varieties of the same, employed chiefly in florid tracery.

k, a pointed arch, formed by the crossing of straight lines, the curves being drawn through the intersections, by the hand.

l, m, & n, are four-centred obtuse arches, the centres of which are upon the diagonal lines, which are formed by dividing the base line into more or less parts, according to the height intended.

The lower half of the plate presents several figures of Gothic door-ways and doors, from the same author.

o, south door-way of Tattershall Church. The waving line across the bottom, shews the plan of the mouldings. One half only is laid down in the plate, the other half being precisely in the same form. The date of this building is A. D. 1455.

p, door-way from Oultin, Norfolk.

q, door-way from Horn Church, Essex, A. D. 1440. Fig. *s*. shews the ground plan of the same.

r, door of the refectory of St. George's Chapel, Windsor.

PLATE II.

aa, specimen of panel from St. Paul's Chapel, Westminster Abbey.
pp, " from Henry the Seventh's Chapel.
oo, " from the monument of Henry IV, in Westminster Abbey.
rr, " from Bishop Longland's Chapel, Lincoln Cathedral.
ss, " from the same.
qq, " from the same.
ff, " from the same.
kk, " from Magdalen College.
mm, " from the palace of Hampton Court.

bb, a Gothic cross, in the florid style.

dd, buttress and pinnacle, at Oxford.

gg, finish of one of the small turrets of the palace at Hampton Court.

ee, niche, or tabernacle and canopy of a buttress, from the South side of Magdalen Church, Oxford. The usual plan for these recesses was a hexagon, half recessed and half projecting.

ll, finial over the door-way of St. Stephen's Chapel, Westminster Abbey.

nn, niche of Bishop Beauchamp, from St. George's Chapel, Windsor, shewing the crocketted canopy, with its finial.

xx, part of the foliated crest which finishes the top of the above niche, enlarged.

tt, finial, from Corpus Christi College.

uu, finial, from Brazen Nose College, Oxford.

34   EXPLANATION OF THE PLATES.

vv, plan of the tracery of the ceiling in the aile of Henry the Seventh's Chapel, shewing one fourth of a compartment.

ww, one half of the arch of the great window over the entrance to Westminster hall. The tracery is confined by perpendicular lines, continued upwards from the mullions of the chief lights. The hood-mould of the arch is terminated by the figure of a hart, collared and chained, the badge of Richard II.

PLATE III.

aaa, elevation of Chancel, drawn for St. Paul's Church, Burlington, Vt. shewing the pulpit with its canopy, the desk, the communion table, the chairs, and the doors immediately behind them, leading into the vestry room.

bbb, section of the above, shewing the canopy over the pulpit, the desk, the altar, the Chancel railing, and the steps, according to their several projections.

ccc, ground plan of the same. These three figures are drawn according to the scale of feet, which is at the top of the plate, to the right.

ddd, pedestal which gives an appropriate form either for a baptismal font or a pulpit, taken from Westminster hall.

eee, canopy for a pulpit or a niche, from All Soul's College, Oxford.

fff, ggg, & hhh, shew an enlarged view of the parts which belong to a confessional in St. Mary's Church, Oxford.

iii, one half of a window from King's College Chapel, Cambridge.

kkk, turret from the entrance tower of Brazen nose College, Oxford.

lll, turret, with a niche below, from the same.

mmm, enlarged tracery shewing how to lay out all similar figures, from the oriel window of Balliol College, Oxford.

PLATE IV.

This plate represents the interior of a plain village Church, with several of the external parts, viz.

A, section of the end which contains the tower, shewing the frame-work o the roof, the belfry, the stairs leading to the same; the organ gallery with an appropriate organ case, the doors below, opening into the vestibule, the two front windows, and the Gothic pilasters, with the Gothic arches, connecting them, and terminating in the main arch of the ceiling.

In this plan, the tower contains the vestibule and the stairs ascending to the organ gallery and belfry, in the first story: in the second story it is divided by a partition into two portions, of which the front portion contains the stairs ascending to the belfry, and the other portion contains the organ gallery as shewn in the plate. Its third story, also shewn in the plate, contains another flight of stairs, above which is the platform where the frame-work for the bell should be placed. The windows opposite the bell may be left open, as represented in the plate, but they look much better closed with boards, planed very thin, not less than five or six inches wide, and about the same distance apart, set in the manner of a Venetian blind, sloping downwards at an angle of about forty-five degrees, and painted a dark stone color. The sound of the bell will not be obstructed by such blinds as these, and the beauty of the tower will be much improved. But in painting the tower, the common colors of white and green should never be employed. Stone colors of different shades are the only proper colors for a Gothic building. See on this subject, Chapter VI.

B. This figure shews a section of the chancel and of the interior, with the frame work of the roof, the end windows, the Gothic pilasters connected with their arches, as before; the pulpit, from the centre of which, at each side, a Gothic screen extends to the end of the chancel railing, and is then turned at right angles to the wall, forming an enclosure for the steps which descend to the vestry room in the basement story, and also for those which ascend to the pulpit. Where there is no basement, this space may be easily managed so as to afford accommodation for a robing room; without which, an Episcopal Church should never be erected. Below the pulpit, is seen the desk; on each side of which, are the doors of the screen. Below the desk appears the communion table, and at each end of the chancel, is a gothic chair. In front, is the chancel railing, in the centre of which is placed the font for baptism. The wall behind and above the screen shews an appropriate finish, which may be given by painting; the two oblong squares representing tablets containing the Lord's prayer, the Creed, the ten commandments, or any other parts of Scripture, according to the choice of the minister; and the centre of the wall exhibiting the sentence, HOLINESS TO THE LORD, or any other short and impressive text, in larger characters. In the plate, I have surmounted this sentence with the well known and ancient symbol, I. H. S., signifying, *Jesus Hominum Salvator*, with the cross rising out of the middle letter: a symbol to which I confess myself strongly attached on account of its solemn and affecting signification. Many pious people are afraid of this figure of the cross, because it is used so extensively by the Church of Rome; but this is a weak and unworthy argument for laying aside any thing, which, in itself, possesses an edifying and wholesome character. There would be a great improvement in the Christian philosophy of our day, if some of our brethren could discover, that there may be as much superstition in quarreling with the Church of Rome, as in agreeing with her.

C. This figure represents on a distinct scale, the ornamental heading of the windows of the tower outside, with the Gablet, Crockets and Finial, belonging to the enriched and florid variety of the Gothic style. They may be carved at an expense which would not exceed forty or fifty dollars for the whole four windows; and they may also be cast in lead or pewter, and nailed on. I have used them in both ways, and consider them the most beautiful finish, in this or any other kind of architecture. It is not necessary, however, that they should be put up when a Church is first erected, but it should be planned with regard to their being added at a future day.

D. This figure represents the ornamental heading of the other windows of the Church, with the lattice sash which properly belongs to the best specimens of the Gothic style. When these can be cast in lead, they should be much smaller than is here represented; but when they are of wood, they cannot be conveniently made, in most cases, of a size much less than the ordinary window sash. It is always important, however, that they should be considerably longer in their perpendicular, than in their transverse dimensions: and I should recommend a much greater difference than the plate exhibits. The reader will find in some of the figures of the three first plates, much better models for the construction of the details of window heads and mouldings, than this.

E. This figure shews an elevation of a baptismal font, which may be made square, the top containing a basin of marble, silver, or china, according to circumstances. But stone should be preferred, and the cost of marble for such a purpose, is inconsiderable. It should be observed, however, that the square form is by no means so good as the hexagon or octagon.

F. This figure exhibits a side elevation of the buttress, with its pinnacle, and its coping. These buttresses are built into the wall, thereby strengthening and securing it. If the Church be of brick, they may be one brick and a half on the face, which face continues the same breadth from the bottom to the top. Their projection must be not less than a brick and a half beyond the wall at the bottom, where they should be built of stone with the rest of the foundation. At the water table where the stone work of a brick edifice usually terminates, the buttresses fall back half a brick in the form of a coping as represented in the plate: see the sections marked A and B. And opposite to the middle part of the wall, or a little below it, they fall back another half brick, leaving a projection of the remaining half brick to continue up to the top of the wall, and then extending inwards upon the wall, they are carried up to a height sufficient for the battlements, and a little above the top of the battlements, as in the plate, they finish square, a brick and a half each way, ending with a pinnacle. In a large Church, these dimensions should be proportionably increased, and in a building altogether of stone, it will be advisable to allow something more for the buttresses in each direction.

I have been thus particular, because the buttresses are an indispensable feature in the Gothic style, and workmen are in need of minute instruction in regard to them, because they are not of frequent occurrence in our country.

The copings where the buttresses fall back, should be of stone below; but above, where they have nothing to bear but the weather, they may be of wood, built in, and painted to agree with the rest of the wall. Their form in such case is marked in fig. F, by dotted lines; but the projection of the outward slope which casts off the water, ought to have a groove or channel *below*, which the plate should have represented.

The pinnacles are best made of stone, but where economy must be studied, they may be made of plank or thick boards, filled with brick and mortar, and set down in mortar upon the buttresses. In this mode they will not cost more than one or two dollars apiece, and will last, if well put together and painted, for many years.

G. This figure represents the organ gallery of fig. A on a larger scale, so as to shew distinctly the top of a plain single Gothic pillar, with the corner and pinnacle above, and the panel work, the battlement, and the connexion of the arch beneath. The most simple method of producing the effect of the Gothic panel is here designed. The front of the gallery is first wainscotted, leaving a sufficient projection to the corner posts for the subsequent finish, then the panels are cut out separately, each being a distinct piece: the inner edge is chamfered three quarters of an inch each way, and the panels thus prepared, are nailed side by side upon the wainscotting. A fillet of about an inch square is then nailed over the joints, intersecting with the same above and below, as in the plate. The same plan is applicable to the panel of the arch, the corner post, &c. the screen behind the pulpit, and every other part where the effect to be produced is similar. The thicker the plank out of which the panel is cut, the richer will be the effect, but a full inch board will look well, and the appearance of it when finished, will be greatly improved, by painting the inside or bottom of the wainscotting, two or three shades darker than the rest; as in the plate. This minute detail may appear trifling, but it must be remembered that I am not writing for architects, nor for men of taste and science in this branch of the arts, but for the clergy who may never have paid the attention of a moment to the subject, until, in some distant region of our extensive country, they are called upon to preside over the erection of a Church, with none but ordinary house carpenters around them. To men thus circumstanced, my own experience of such little difficulties is a sufficient proof that these practical hints will be valuable. I furnish them for this reason, without any regard to the criticisms of those for whom they were not intended. Utility, not fame, is my object. Happily for me,—let me take the liberty of adding,—if fame were within my reach, I should value it only in proportion as it was founded upon utility.

PLATE V.

This plate represents a perspective view of Trinity Church, Pittsburgh, the building mentioned in the preface, as being the first fruits of the necessity which turned my attention to the study of Church architecture. The best part of the exterior of this building is the tower, which exhibits an example of the flying buttress, taken from Henry the Seventh's Chapel. The pinnacles of the tower are finished with crockets and finials, or *purfled*, according to the phraseology of the Gothic style.

Fig. 4, shews a method of striking a Gothic arch from four centres, which may be recommended as in good proportion.

Fig. 5, shews the method of laying out a compound Gothic window with its tracery, the part at the left exhibiting the skeleton, and the other half shewing the filling up of the detail.

Fig. 6, shews the base and the capital of a single Gothic pillar, taken from St. George's Chapel, Windsor.

Fig. 7, shews the flying buttress on a larger scale.

Fig. 8, shews a pendant of the ceiling, taken from Crosby hall, London.

PLATE VI.

Fig. 9. This figure represents, according to the scale below, an arrangement of the chancel, in which the pulpit and the desk are at each side, and the altar in the middle, with a richly ornamented Gothic window over it. Between the window and the buttresses at the sides, are tablets, containing sentences from Scripture;

under which are the chairs. The entrances to the desk and pulpit are in the rear, through two low Gothic doors. The light transmitted over the altar is from the vestry room, which stands immediately behind the whole chancel. There are canopies over the pulpit and desk, on each side of which rises a buttress enriched in the florid style, taken from Henry the Seventh's Chapel. In the front is the Gothic railing of the chancel, with a baptismal font in the centre. Upon this plan the pulpit and desk are in the same form, the pulpit being only a little higher.

Fig. 10. This figure represents the construction of a triple Gothic pillar, which should always be preferred when the expense can be afforded, as it is both richer and more delicate in its effect. There is a fault in the plate, however, which must be carefully avoided. The circles are too large. Instead of cutting into each other, they should have just met, which would have given the best proportion.

Fig. 11, shews a good form for a Gothic pulpit.

Fig. 14, another for the same.

Fig. 15, shews the enriched buttress used in No. 9, on a larger scale.

Fig. 17, shews the railing of the chancel in No. 9. on a larger scale.

Fig. 13. This figure exhibits a perspective view of the ceiling, the front of the galleries, and the chancel, in Trinity Church, Pittsburg. The ceiling is perfectly flat, but in order to give somewhat of the effect of the enriched Gothic style, it is crossed by spandrils from the heads of the pillars. Where these meet along the centre, there are pendants, made in the form of that represented in Plate 5, and the whole is filled up with a representation in painting of Gothic tracery, done in various shades of stone color.

When fresh, and for several years afterwards, this kind of finish looks extremely well, if skilfully executed; because it gives an accurate picture of the exquisite fretwork of the English Gothic Churches. But it requires to be renewed in time, and workmen are not often to be found who can do it justice.

Fig. 12, represents the head of one of the pillars with its spandrils, as in No. 13, but on a larger scale.

Fig. 16, shews the plan of the ceiling in No. 13, the part at the left exhibiting the skeleton, and that, at the right, shewing the filling up, in imitation of fretwork.

Fig. 19, shews the border of foliage which surrounds the oval and the segments of circles in No. 16, on a larger scale. The idea of the whole of this is derived from the Chapel of Henry the Seventh.

Fig. 18, a perspective view of the battlements which finish the top of the galleries in Trinity Church, Pittsburgh.

PLATE VII.

The principal figure in this plate represents a perspective view of a design for a Gothic Church, with an octagonal steeple, instead of a tower. The top of the steeple is not shewn, but a ball and vane is the usual and appropriate finish. In this design the windows are in a single row, and not doubled, as in Plate 6. And therefore this design is better, because it accords with the principle set forth in the first chapter; viz. the giving force to the perpendicular line, as far as practicable. The building at the end, is a vestry room, which agrees with the style of the main building, and the window above is to throw light into the chancel, over the altar, where the plan laid down in Plate 6, No. 9, is preferred. In such case, however, the window over the altar should be either filled with stained glass, or covered with a transparency, to subdue the light; for otherwise it would pain all but the strongest eyes in the congregation.

Fig. 21, shews a ground plan with two ailes; but three ailes are better.

A, is the vestibule, containing the stairs to the organ gallery.

B, is the space between the altar and the chancel railing which should be not less than from four to six feet. The centre of the railing shews the place for the baptismal font.

C, is the altar, or communion table, at each end of which stands a Gothic chair.

D & E, the desk and pulpit, both entered from the vestry room behind.

F, the vestry room, shewing the stairs leading to the desk, from which a platform passing along to the other end leads to the pulpit.

Fig. 22. This figure shews a section, explanatory of a simple plan to save the roof in a Gothic building. In order to understand it, the reader will bear in mind that the finishing the wall with a battlement is a constant characteristic of the

Gothic style. This, however, produces what is called by workmen a *valley gutter*: that is, the sloping roof meeting with the wall which forms the battlement, makes a valley, or hollow, from which the water must be carried through pipes to the ground. Now the practical difficulty in this case is, that no degree of care in the construction of these valley gutters, is usually able to keep them from leaking. In the summer half of the year, they do well enough; but in winter, the freezing and thawing of the snow upon the roof, almost invariably produces leakage, which ruins, in time, the ceiling below, occasions the plaster to crack and fall down, and makes the building both unsafe and unsightly.

The mode in which I think the whole of this difficulty can be avoided, is shewn in the fig. marked 22, which is a section exhibiting the wall, the roof, the eave-trough, and the battlement, as follows, viz.

a, the wall;

b, the roof;

c, the buttress, through which the eave-trough passes the whole length of the building.

d, the plank which forms the battlement, which is spiked or screwed to the eave-trough in such a manner, that the openings or embrasures of the battlement are a little below the edge of the eave-trough. The triangular piece which projects backward from this plank, is merely to give the appearance of thickness from below; without which, the battlement would seem to want substance.

e, the eave-trough, hollowed, as usual, out of solid timber, and having the outer edge an inch lower than the inner. The piece of plank below the trough, is for ornament, as is also the fillet outside; and the appearance of the whole is shewn accurately in the perspective view above it, in the same plate.

The operation of this is, that the battlement does not form a valley at all. It is not, as in the ordinary cases, a continuation of the wall; but it is attached to the eave-trough: and whenever the eave-trough fills in frosty weather, and a thaw succeeds, the openings of the battlement, being as low, or a little lower than the outer edge of the eave-trough, afford an escape for the water, which effectually prevents its rising above the edge of the roof, and flowing inwards upon the wall. It is cheaper than the other method, because the application of tin or lead to the valley gutter is rendered unnecessary; and the beauty of the effect is so far from being diminished by the projecting of the battlement outwards, that I think it is rather increased. Care, however, must be taken to have the buttresses project sufficiently to allow of this finish, without having any part of the work to come within an inch of their face. The inspection of the perspective view marked No. 20, will make this plain.

PLATE VIII.

THE figure in the plate, marked No. 23, exhibits the front view of the same building of which the rear was presented in Plate 7. The upper part of the steeple is quite too short for a proper proportion, and should be about twice as high from the base of the pyramid to the top. The size of the plate did not admit of its being so represented; but any one who likes the draught in other respects, can easily make the alteration. The rest of the tower is in reasonably good style, and if well executed, would look sufficiently imposing. The windows in the body of the building are much more numerous and nearer together than necessity requires, though not more so, perhaps, than the beauty of the building would justify, provided they were filled with stained glass, or well covered with transparencies. Their number, however, can be diminished, at pleasure.

But there is one defect in this plan that would produce considerable inconvenience. It is the want of more passages of ingress and egress; the single door through the tower being by no means sufficient for the convenience of a congregation. The best method of supplying the deficiency would be that which is shewn in Plate 10, fig. 25.

PLATE IX.

THIS plate presents a perspective drawing of a design for a small cathedral, in which the roof is concealed by a rich screen of tracery, the water, however, having the same means of escape provided as formerly described, through the lower row of small Gothic arches. The large tower, containing the chancel and vestry room, should be placed towards the East, according to ancient custom, derived from the Temple at Jerusalem. And two doors, one at each side of the tower would be necessary, in addition to the western door, shewn in the plate, for the ingress and egress of the congregation. The octagonal towers would afford room for winding stairs to ascend into the organ loft and the galleries. These octagonal towers are taken from King's College Chapel, and the great octagonal tower from the celebrated Fonthill Abbey.

PLATE X.

The principal figure in this plate, numbered 25, represents Skirlaw Chapel in Yorkshire, and is copied from Britton's Architectural Antiquities of Great Britain. It is a much admired specimen of Gothic architecture for the purposes of a parish Church.

Fig. 26, represents a quatre foil opening, from Red Mount Chapel, Lynn, Norfolk.
Fig. 27, exhibits a font from Binham Priory Church, Norfolk.
Fig. 28, shews the capital and base of a Gothic pillar from Red Mount Chapel.

PLATE XI.

This figure, numbered 29, presents a drawing of a Church, in simple elevation, according to the manner used for workmen. The scale is one tenth of an inch to the foot.

PLATE XII.

The principal figure in this plate, No. 30, shews the front elevation, and fig. 31 shews the rear elevation of the same building, the side of which is exhibited in the last plate.

Fig. 32, is a perspective drawing, taken from Britton, of St. Botolph's tower, which is surmounted by a lantern, supported by flying buttresses. It is a remarkable example of the kind.

PLATE XIII.

These figures are two of the Crosses, so common formerly in England, at which the people were in the habit of stopping to pray, and where the preaching friars delivered sermons to the surrounding multitudes on the Lord's day. I have added them to this little work, partly as an interesting relic of former days, but more because I think they might furnish beautiful models for Gothic monuments, in commemoration of 'the dead, who die in the Lord.'

The figure on the left is the Cross at Leighton Buzzard, Bedfordshire; and that, on the right, represents the Cross at Winchester, Hampshire. This last is $43\frac{1}{2}$ feet high.

There is, on the frontispiece, a representation of another,—the Black-Friars' Cross, at Hereford—which, though in ruin, retains enough of its original character to afford a useful example of the Gothic style.

CONCLUDING OBSERVATIONS.

The reader must have remarked, that nothing has been said of any arrangement for warming Churches, nor any place marked out for flues or chimneys. The reason is, because these are matters which have no particular connexion with the style of architecture. Chimneys are deformities in every public edifice, and all that can be done, so long as they are necessary, is to dispose of them where they shall attract the smallest possible observation. In the Gothic style, however, the buttresses afford an opportunity for carrying up flues with great convenience, and by making the pinnacles of those buttresses of cast iron, with the opening at the side which is farthest from the spectator, the whole purposes of chimneys may be provided for, without any violation of good taste. And where this plan may not be thought advisable, the chimney may be so designed as to resemble a turret, with battlements above, and thus be kept in consistency with the style of building.

As to the modes of applying heat for the purpose of warming Churches, it is

CONCLUSION.

beside the object of this little work to enlarge upon them. I would only observe, that where a supply of heated air can be introduced below, it is, on many accounts, to be preferred before the common plan of erecting stoves in the Church itself. Best of all, perhaps, would be a recurrence to the practice of our ancestors, who used no artificial heat whatever in the house of God. But if this be too much to expect from the effeminacy of our day, it might be well to consider whether the end could not be sufficiently accomplished by conducting, at the side of each aile, a stove pipe, made square, instead of round, and secured by brick or stone work so as to form a part of the floor of the building.

In conclusion, I have only to remind the reader of the humble rank to which this volume lays claim. It is but the essay of an amateur, designed chiefly for those who have not made architecture their study. No man can be more sensible than myself, of its defects; yet, well knowing the want of some plain and simple directory of the kind, I lay it upon the altar of utility with the hope that it may be found acceptable to some of my brethren, and save them from many of those perplexities which commonly attend an attempt to erect the earthly sanctuary of God. With regard to credit, emolument, or reputation, I may well apply the adage, 'Happy is he that expecteth nothing, for he shall not be disappointed.' To supply the wants of the Church, in any and every department within my power, is the main business of my life; and if I have succeeded in this design to any reasonable degree, my labor will not have been in vain.

Errata.—In page 13, line 15 from top, for 'If' read 'In.'
" 23, line 12, " for 'carved' read 'curved.'
" 25, line 6, " for 'Bay-windows' read 'Bay-window.'
" 35, line 3, " for 'o' read 'of.'
" 41, line 9, " for 'Plate 6' read 'Plate 5.'

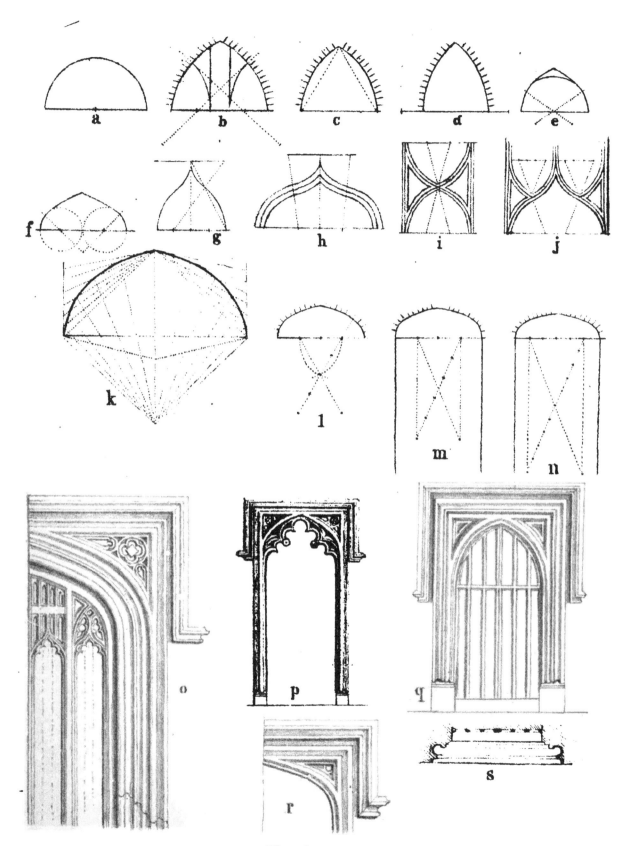

Plate 1.

Plate 2.

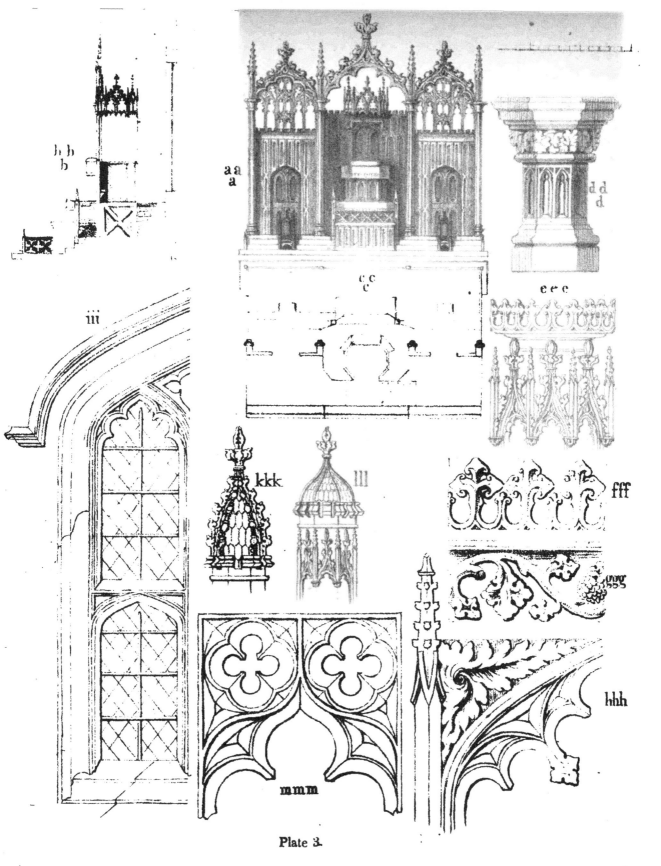

Plate 3.

Plate 4.

Plate 5.

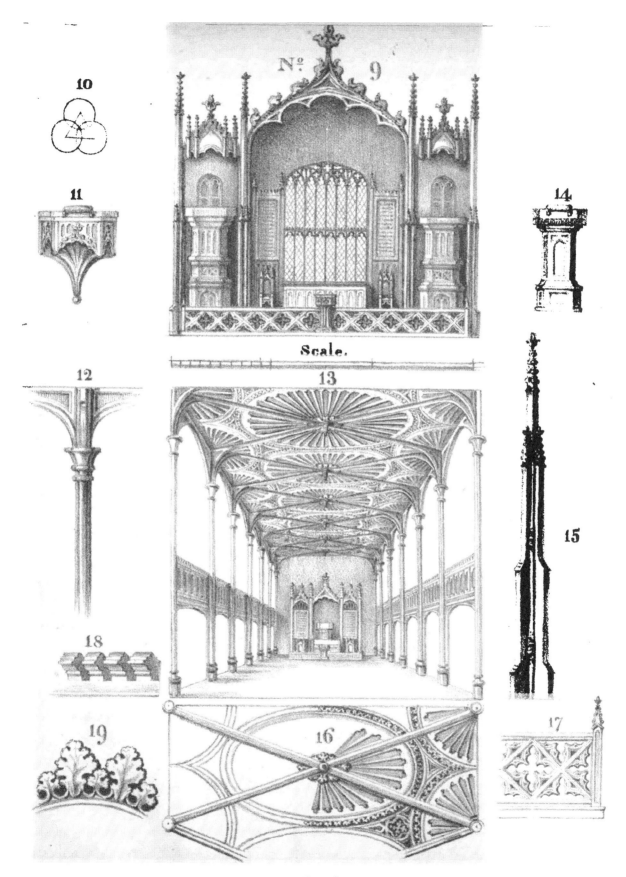

Plate 6.

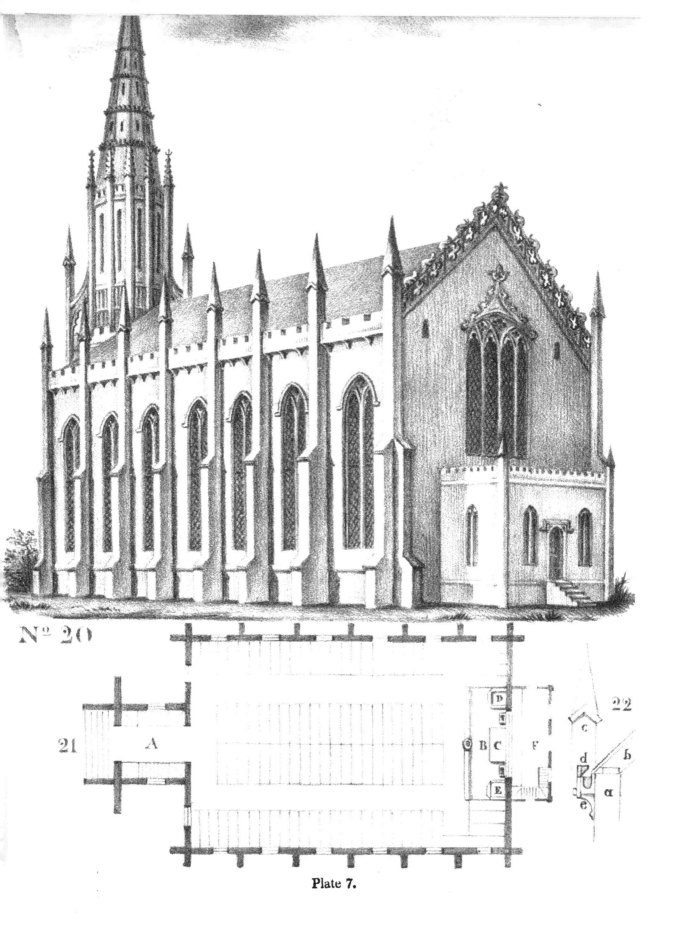

N° 20

21   A

22

Plate 7.

Nº 24

Plate 9.

Nº 25

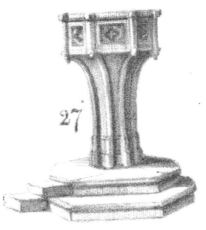

Plate IV.

N⁰ 29

Plate 11.

Plate 12.

Plate 13.

CPSIA information can be obtained at www.ICGtesting.com
Printed in the USA
LVOW011607241112

308652LV00005B/113/P

9 781174 885945